In the Days of the Dinosaurs

A Troop of Little Dinosaurs

Story by Hugh Price
Illustrations by Ben Spiby

One day, Little Dinosaur was swept away down the river in a flood.
When at last he struggled back to dry land, he was lost, and far from home.

He was tired, too,
but he could not rest for long
because he had to keep watching
for Big Dinosaur, his terrible enemy.

Little Dinosaur had hurt his leg.
It was stiff and sore,
and he could not run fast.
He would not be able to escape
if Big Dinosaur found him now.

As Little Dinosaur limped along,
he tried to keep out of sight
down in the ferns and the undergrowth.
He was scared.
The world was full of danger.

Then he heard a noise! What was it?
Little Dinosaur stopped and listened.
He smelled the air.

When Little Dinosaur looked through the ferns,
he saw some other little dinosaurs.
They were just like him!

But would they be friends... or enemies?

The little dinosaurs were scratching about
on the ground and turning over stones
as they hunted for things to eat.

Little Dinosaur kept very still as he watched them.

Suddenly, the troop of little dinosaurs
turned to face him. They had seen him.

Little Dinosaur was frightened. He stepped back.

But instead of attacking him,
the oldest dinosaur lifted her head.

She could smell danger on the wind!
She knew that Big Dinosaur,
with his sharp and terrible teeth, was coming.
The oldest dinosaur hit her tail on the ground
to warn the troop.   *Run!*

All the little dinosaurs turned
and fled into the forest.
Little Dinosaur limped after them
as fast as he could.
He had to struggle to keep the others in sight.

When at last they all stopped running,
Big Dinosaur, their terrible enemy,
had been left a long way behind.

They were safe again... for a while.

After that, Little Dinosaur was never far away
from the troop of dinosaurs.
He did not go too close to them,
but he did not let them out of his sight, either.
If he stayed near them he felt safe,
because **all** the troop kept watch.

Together, the troop of little dinosaurs
had **nine** pairs of eyes to watch for enemies,
nine pairs of ears for listening,
and **nine** long noses for smelling the wind.

In the days that followed,
Little Dinosaur's stiff leg began to get better.
The other dinosaurs grew used
to seeing him nearby,
and no one chased him away.

Then, one day, Little Dinosaur was the first
to smell Big Dinosaur coming.
He was the first to give the warning thump.
The troop all raced off together.

Now there were
ten dinosaurs to keep watch,
thanks to Little Dinosaur.

Big Dinosaur, with his sharp and terrible teeth, would **never** be able to get close to him again. Little Dinosaur belonged to the troop, and he felt safe, at last.